EAT YOUR
SUPERPOWERS!

Many thanks to Jaimie Winkler, RDN,
for her ready clarification and professional
guidance as we created this book.
www.jaimiewinkler.com

RISE x Penguin Workshop
An imprint of Penguin Random House LLC, New York

First published in the United States of America by Rise × Penguin Workshop,
an imprint of Penguin Random House LLC, New York, 2023

Text copyright © 2023 by Toni Buzzeo
Illustrations copyright © 2023 by Serge Bloch

PENGUIN is a registered trademark and PENGUIN WORKSHOP is a trademark of Penguin Books Ltd.
The W and RISE Balloon colophons are registered trademarks of Penguin Random House LLC.

Visit us online at penguinrandomhouse.com.

Library of Congress Cataloging-in-Publication Data is available.

Manufactured in China

ISBN 9780593522950   10 9 8 7 6 5 4 3 2 1   HH

The text is set in Helvetica LT Pro Condensed.
The art was created with photography, pen, and humor . . .

Edited by Cecily Kaiser
Designed by Maria Elias

EAT YOUR SUPERPOWERS!

How Colorful Foods Keep You Healthy and Strong

written by Toni Buzzeo

pictures by Serge Bloch

RISE

NEW YORK

For Elsie,
intrepid taster of new foods.
—TB

TABLE OF CONTENTS

INTRODUCTION

When you look at the fruits, vegetables, nuts,

and grains that you eat, how many different

colors do you see? Do you ever wonder why?

Tiny nutrients in plants give them their colors

and protect them from becoming sick. Those

same nutrients can help our bodies and protect

us from getting sick, too. Each tasty, colorful

food has work to do inside our bodies.

Learn how each food can give you

SUPERPOWERS—helping you stay strong,

healthy, smart, and full of energy.

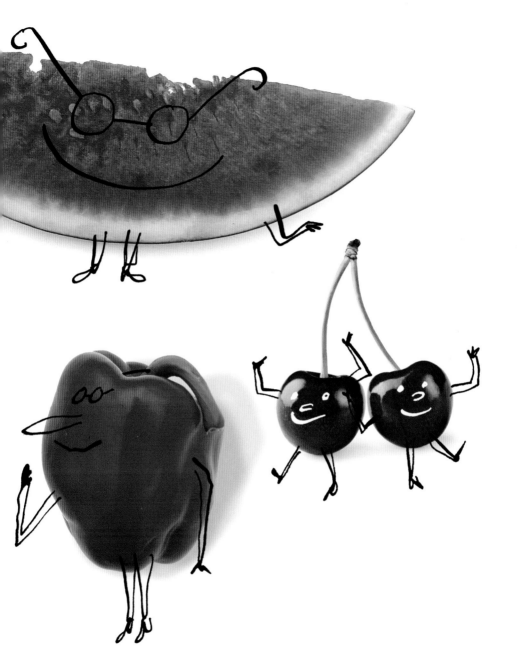

RED & PINK FOODS

RED GRAPES

help you fight drippy,
sneezy allergies.

quercetin

TOMATOES
guard your heart
and keep it relaxed.

---

lycopene + potassium

WATERMELON,
sweet and juicy,
helps you stay hydrated.

water

19

RED PEPPERS

help your skin heal sores
and cuts.

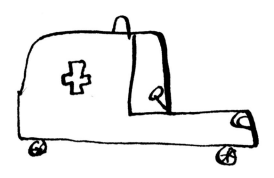

----

vitamin C

CHERRIES

keep your heart beating
in a steady bah-bum,
bah-bum rhythm.

———

potassium

24

ORANGE

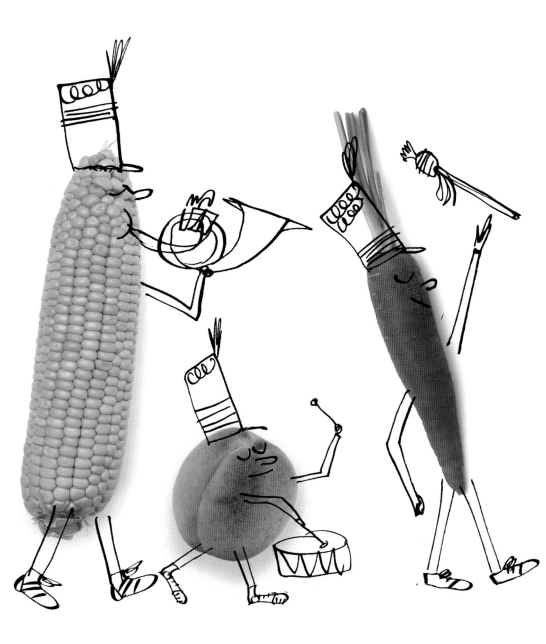

& YELLOW FOODS

BANANAS

keep your muscles strong
so that you can easily move
your body.

---

potassium

CORN

helps your body turn other
foods you eat into energy.

vitamin B$_1$

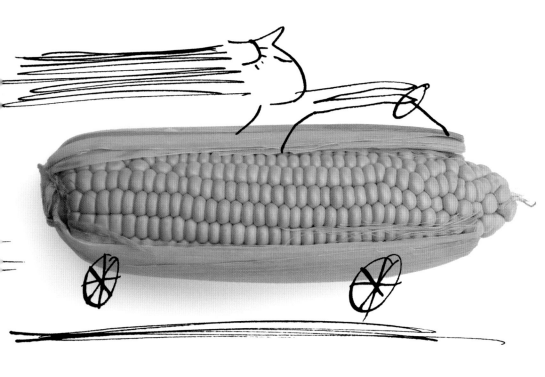

APRICOTS

keep your skin smooth
and soft.

---

vitamins A, C, K

SWEET POTATOES

help you grow healthy hair
and strong fingernails.

---

vitamin B_7

CARROTS,
crunchy and sweet,
clean your teeth as you eat.

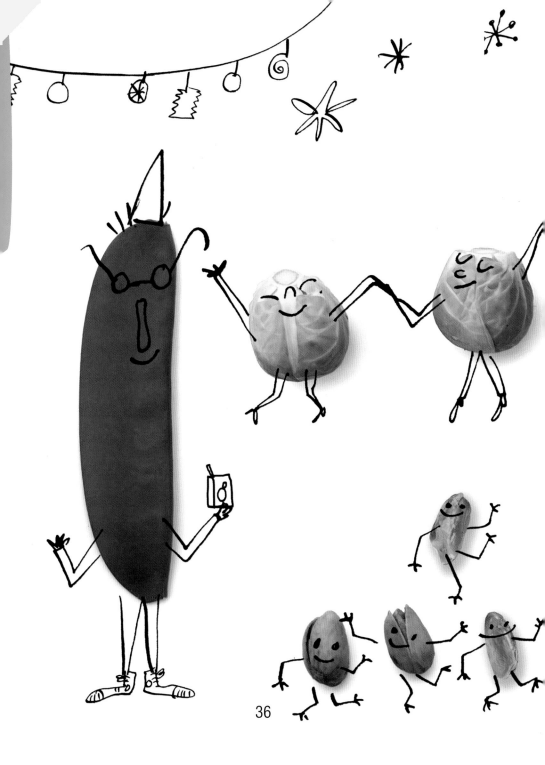

36

GREEN FOODS

SNAP PEAS
help your body
fight off germs.

beta-carotene

PISTACHIOS

protect your eyes
and keep them strong.

lutein + zeaxanthin

BRUSSELS SPROUTS

help your brain move from sadness to happiness.

---

folate

43

KIWIS

help your brain think
quickly and clearly.

---

vitamin C

KALE

helps your skin make
a scab whenever you bleed.

---

vitamin K

BLUE

& PURPLE FOODS

BLUEBERRIES

keep your kidneys strong
so they can turn the liquids
you drink into pee.

---

antioxidants + anthocyanins

PLUMS

help you feel calm
when you are worried.

chlorogenic acid

EGGPLANT

defends your body from sickness.

---

anthocyanins

FIGS

help keep your bones strong and solid.

---

calcium + potassium

57

BEETS

help you breathe lots of air
deep into your lungs.

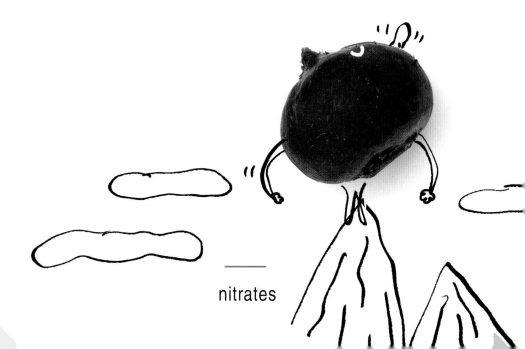

nitrates

59

BROWN

& WHITE FOODS

OATMEAL
fills up your tummy
and helps you poop.

---

fiber

CASHEWS

protect your hearing when sounds around you get too loud.

---

magnesium

WHEAT

helps your body grow.

---

plant protein

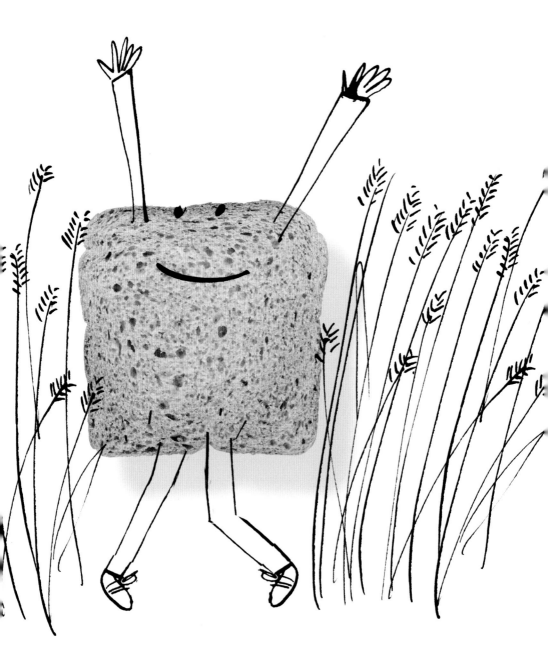

RICE

gives you energy
that lasts all day long.

---

carbohydrates

TOFU

keeps your teeth
healthy and strong.

phosphorus

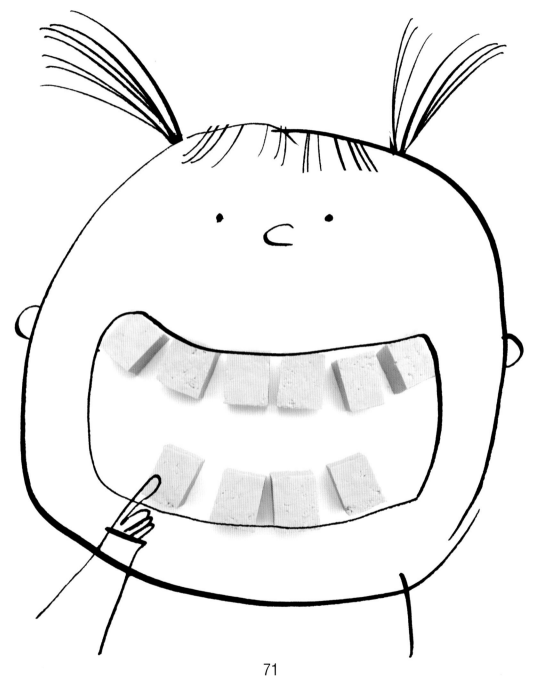

FOOD OPTIONS

Sometimes we don't want to eat (or *can't* eat) a food that is good
for our bodies or our minds. Just in case this happens to you,
check below to find a food option that will help you in the same way!

INSIDE YOUR BODY,
there are two ways to . . .

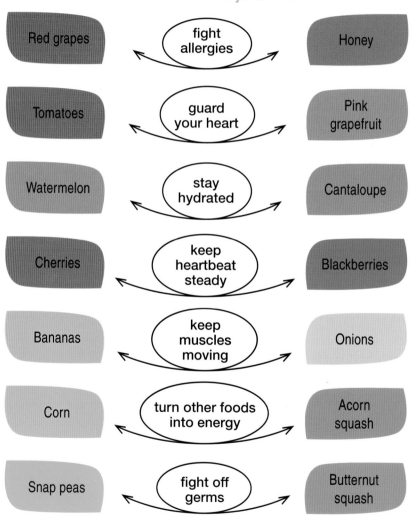

Red grapes	fight allergies	Honey
Tomatoes	guard your heart	Pink grapefruit
Watermelon	stay hydrated	Cantaloupe
Cherries	keep heartbeat steady	Blackberries
Bananas	keep muscles moving	Onions
Corn	turn other foods into energy	Acorn squash
Snap peas	fight off germs	Butternut squash

72

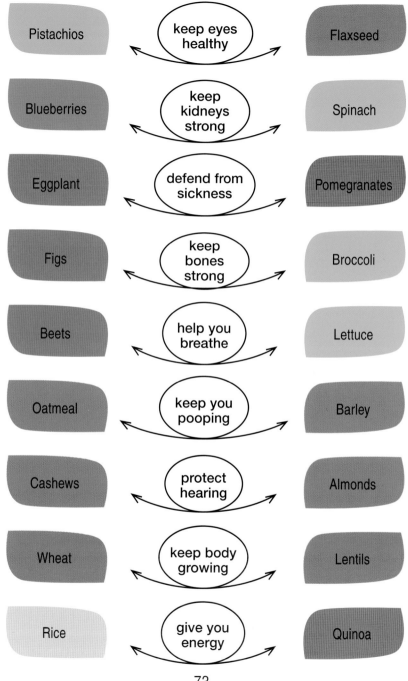

Pistachios	keep eyes healthy	Flaxseed
Blueberries	keep kidneys strong	Spinach
Eggplant	defend from sickness	Pomegranates
Figs	keep bones strong	Broccoli
Beets	help you breathe	Lettuce
Oatmeal	keep you pooping	Barley
Cashews	protect hearing	Almonds
Wheat	keep body growing	Lentils
Rice	give you energy	Quinoa

73

OUTSIDE YOUR BODY,
there are two ways to . . .

Red peppers	heal sores	Raspberries
Apricots	keep skin healthy	Mangoes
Sweet potatoes	grow healthy hair and nails	Peanuts
Carrots	clean teeth	Celery
Kale	help stop bleeding	Strawberries
Tofu	keep teeth strong	Chia seeds

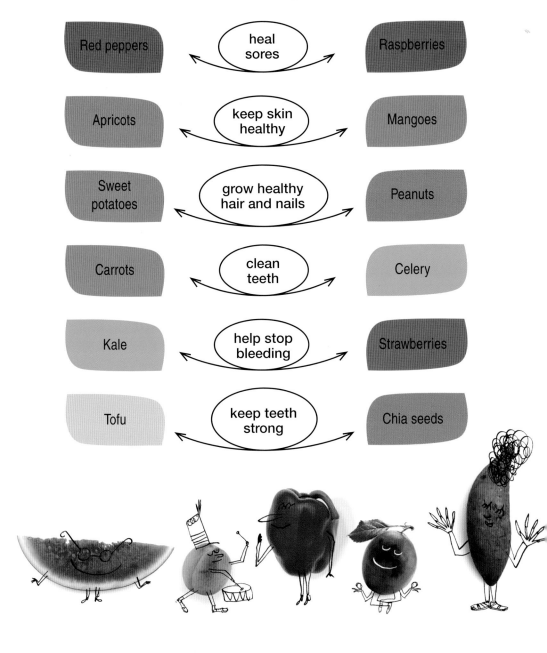

INSIDE YOUR MIND,
there are two ways to . . .

Brussels sprouts	← help your brain to keep you smiling →	Papaya
Kiwis	← keep brain healthy →	Oranges
Plums	← help you stay calm →	Pears

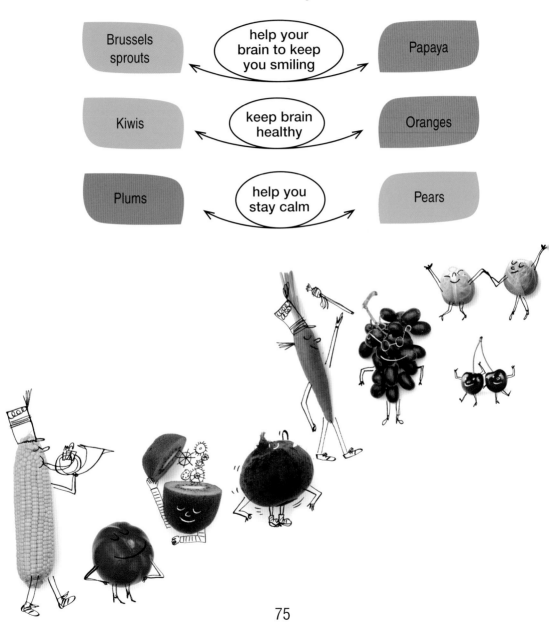

BODY CHART

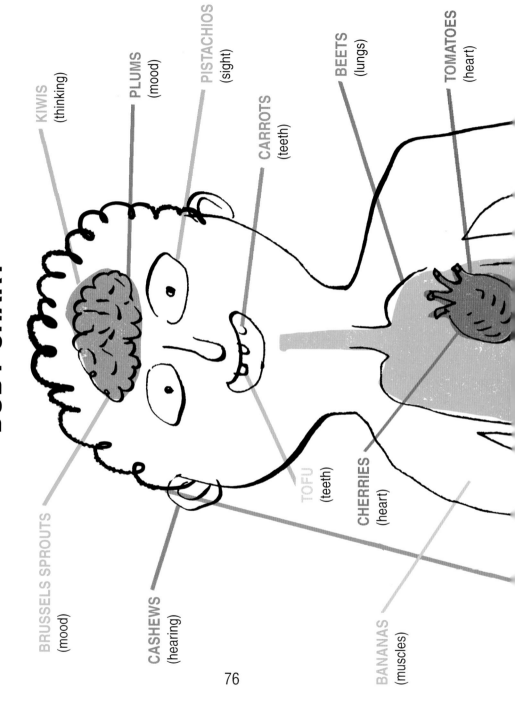

KIWIS
(thinking)

PLUMS
(mood)

PISTACHIOS
(sight)

CARROTS
(teeth)

BEETS
(lungs)

TOMATOES
(heart)

BRUSSELS SPROUTS
(mood)

CASHEWS
(hearing)

TOFU
(teeth)

CHERRIES
(heart)

BANANAS
(muscles)

76

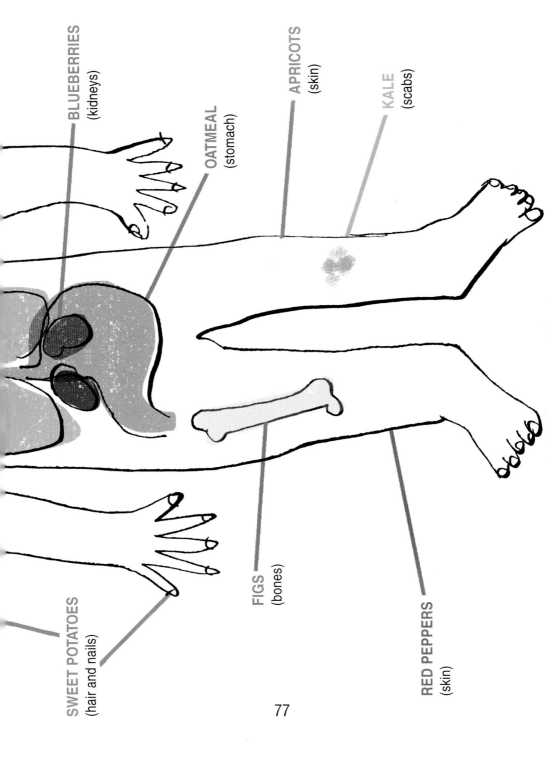

BLUEBERRIES
(kidneys)

OATMEAL
(stomach)

APRICOTS
(skin)

KALE
(scabs)

SWEET POTATOES
(hair and nails)

FIGS
(bones)

RED PEPPERS
(skin)